To Sink, To Rise

Cait Warner

Presentation by *BookLeaf Publishing*

Web: www.bookleafpub.com

E-mail: info@bookleafpub.com

ISBN: 9789360948849

First edition 2024

*For my Mother who deserved tenderness; I
now know the pain you endured.*

*For those who too, sacrificed their peace in
the name of love.*

PREFACE

This is for those who have given their
wholeness, purity and love,
Only to find in return bitterness, betrayal and
sadness.

Do not let the darkness of others dim your light,
though you may feel you have sunk to your
deepest depths, you will always rise again.

To Sink

I want to sink through the floor, letting the
darkness engulf me as I slip quietly from view.

I want to exist off-stage; I no longer want an
audience,
no laughter,
no tears.

So draw the curtains, The show is over;
Desdemona sleeps, our tragedies pre-written,
and I will sink through the floor, slipping quietly
from view.

Carcass

I have just been existing.

The words "I" and "Me" hold no meaning, Who is she?

I never could have imagined the world that is my reality.

I have never been so quiet.

I am faceless, empty, a carcass stuffed full of his venom and knives, I am not allowed to cry.

It hurts, but he says it doesn't; I used to feel.

I am just a carcass existing, surrounded by the perfumes of other girls in my sleep.

I only ever have loved, I only wanted love.

None of this can be real.

Who am I?

This carcass is rotting.

Skin

The stable home I built inside myself was decimated.

I was finally settling into safety, into trust;
But I mistook wolves for dogs.

I took in monsters that now hide in the hollow walls and creep through the empty halls.

I am never safe, I don't feel safe.

They scream over my own thoughts, this house
beneath my skin is theirs;
I have lost all autonomy.

I don't recognize myself in the mirror.

Where did I go?

I want to go to where she is.

Beneath my skin, this house is haunted.

Women

We don't die running away in beautiful dresses
with perfectly tear-stained faces.

We die ripped naked; shaking and bruised,

screaming and screaming and screaming,
and screaming and screaming,

until there is no air left in the world to fill our
lungs and our throats are raw with blood.

I can still taste it.

We die where we should have been loved.

He Buried Me

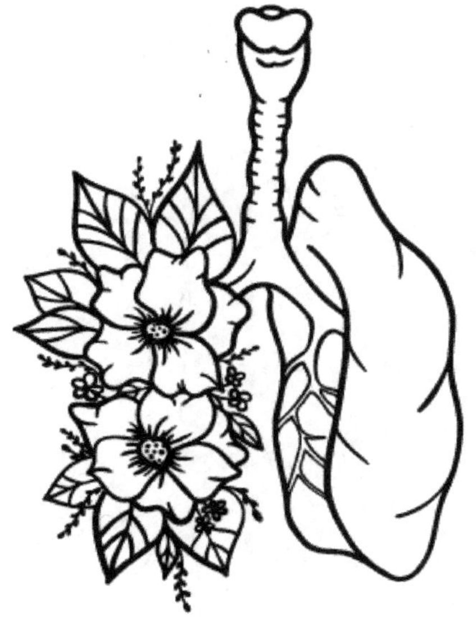

The dirt is damp and cold on my skin,
It fills my lungs and mouth,
I forget what it was like to breathe.

My eyes burn, I forget the sun, I forget me.

Maybe flowers will grow here in time,
where I decay.

Released.

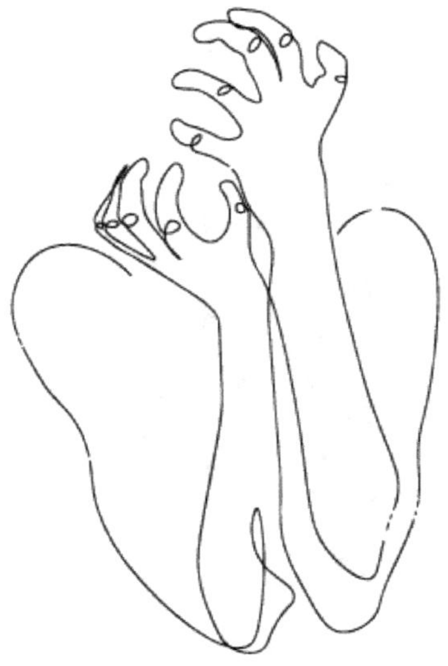

His words were snakes coiling around me,
whispering all I wanted and needed to hear,
rehearsed and poetic;
Constricting my lifeline,
the last things that were keeping who I was,
alive.
I swear I'm not who I became,
he got inside my brain,
his voice ran through the blood in my veins.

I was addicted and sick,
blinded by the absence of my mind.
A zombie, walking only for him.
Standing alone in the shower,
eyes empty,
trying to unfold from the skin he touched,
the skin he tainted.
Never looking in the mirror,
disgusted by the stranger looking back at me.

I wanted to run into the deepest depths of a
forest,
disappear from sight, from everyone.
To scream, to cry until I was released from him.

I'll never know.

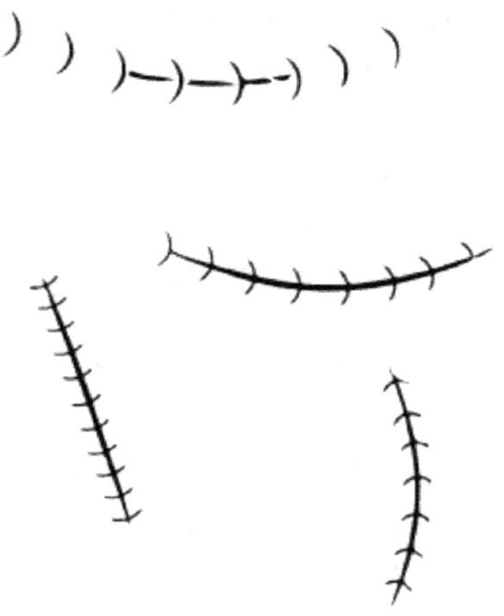

I wonder if I will ever meet the real me.

I wonder who she would have, could have been,
If his hands had never touched me,
If his words had never met my ears,
and his violence;

violence.

Would she ever know such violence?

I am forever changed, I know I am forever
changed.

Chain smoking

Chainsmoking at 7am,
The smell of ash hangs heavy in the air;
The sound of cars becoming more frequent
while my coffee turns cold as I neglect it for
another cigarette.

They burn out quicker than my mind can ease
itself.

The sun rises faster than I can fall asleep.

The world continues on.
It always continues on.

Fear

An ever-quaking entity reverberates in my chest;
it's an echo that follows me wherever I go.

I don't know when it started.

A voice I cannot recall,
I don't know who it belongs to.

It's an uncomfortable familiar;
It feels like everyone I've ever known.

I know there is another way to live.

Finding Myself

This morning I watched the sun rise through
spiderwebs,
They shimmer like golden threads on my garden
gate.

A glimmer.

I feel her in these moments of stillness,
a whisper in the breeze, she tells me I can be her
again.

I want to shed the past like an old skin,
I'll untangle gently, I'll exist in glimmers;
I'll find her there.

A Wish

I wish to be loved gently,
I imagine warmth, I imagine the morning sun,
and the meeting of eyes that linger before the
meeting of lips.

I wish to be held softly,
no expectations, my body only a vessel for my
soul;
the feeling of safety in touch.

I wish to be loved gently,
I wish to be loved truly,

I wish.

Autonomy

I want to be loved without being owned.

I am not your possession.

You do not possess me.

Just love me softly, kindly, let our light naturally
shine through tenderness; like stars or the glow
of the moon behind clouds.

Those that care to look will see effortlessly.

A love that is not curated for stage, artificial
lights and scripted words,

A show for the world to look in on,
A blinding spotlight,
Only to prove that I am yours.

I want to be loved without being owned.

Purge.

Today I cried.

Two years' worth of tears I was never allowed to
let fall.

Two years' worth of tears I had learned were
safer to swallow.

I cried so much I was sick.

Maybe this is how I expel the pain.

A Realisation.

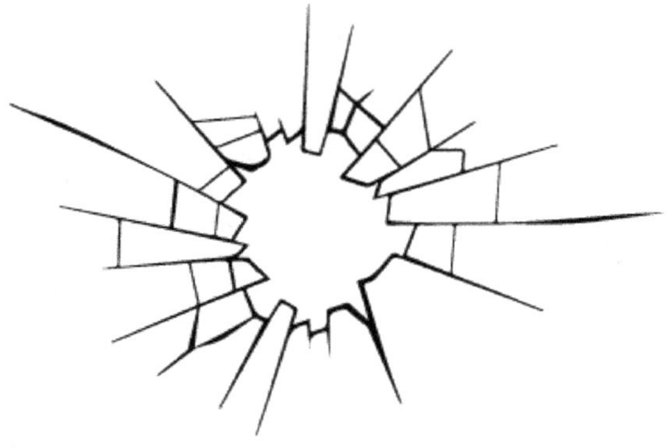

This was never my war,
I got caught in the crossfire between you and
your own reflection.

Peace

I can't live in your world any longer.
There is no peace here.

I want to, I need to live in mine.
It was so full of peace; In peace is how I exist,
but here,
you will not let me.

I gave everything to survive in your world,
I sacrificed my peace for my love;
but now I must save what little I have left of
myself.

I will exist in peace again.

I Am

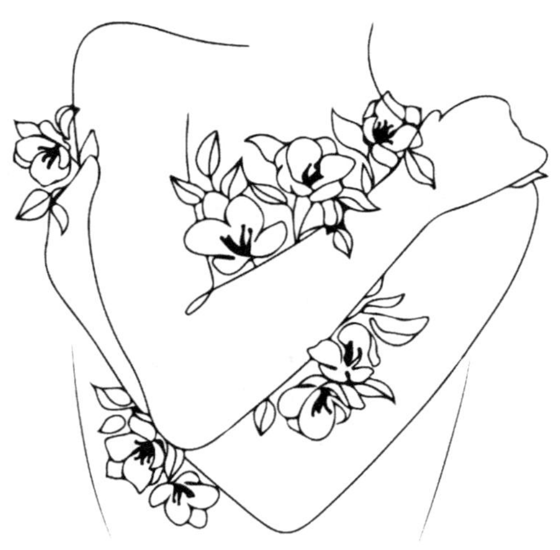

I am wildflowers,
sunrises and sunsets,
I am gentle winds and softly spoken words,
summer dresses on a warm summer's day,
and the reflections of stars in the ripples of lakes
at night.

I am wildflowers;
You can not tell me when, or how I should
bloom.
I belong to myself alone.

Rest

We have danced for too long, let us breathe in
the last of December's air and exhale the past;
Let us finally rest, we have worn down our
shoes and the music has slowed.

Maybe now we will have time to watch the
sunrise from northern shores, with no fear of the
coming day.

We have danced for too long, let us lay under the
stars and inhale the universe as it turns above us;
All the beauty in the world awaiting us, let it
wrap us in comfort, we have struggled for too
long.

Everything Is Temporary

Blue skies with clouds softly laying upon the
horizon,
pull my soul just past their sun-coated glow,
leaving my weighted body longing to follow.

The silhouettes of birds fill my empty shell,
as they glide over the world far past where I
have ever been,
I can only ever watch as they leave.

One day I will follow them there.

Acceptance.

The rain fell hard upon my skin, but I walked
slowly in it,
taking in the world as I went upon my way.

Inner Child

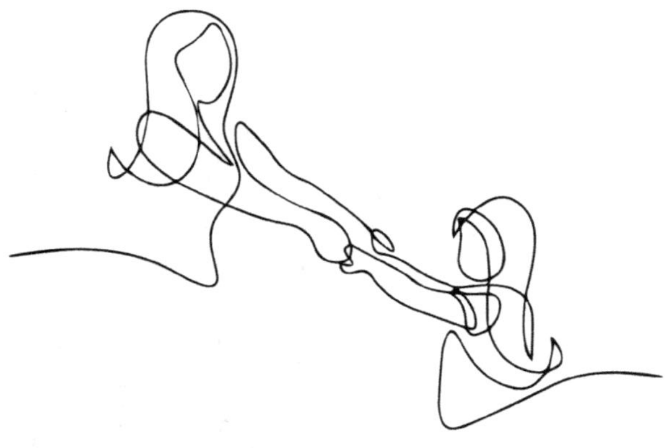

Sitting in my own home,
Alone on the kitchen bench,
I am warmer now, though my hands are still cold
and shake sometimes,
I know now that there is always a new morning,
there is always an after.

The scent of a baking cake fills the air here,
I am safe in this home that I have built.

I am friends with the girl in the mirror now,
I hold the pain of the girl she was in my arms,
I nurture her, I love her for being so strong when
she was so young;
she waded through trauma to arrive in this place
where I can comfort her,

my inner child.

I don't blame her for the scars on our skin,
nor the time she spent screaming at the world,
the nights spent in the cold.

I have grown into the woman she wished she
had to turn to,
into the friend she cried herself to sleep for.
She rose up from the cold kitchen floor so I
could be here.

I will do the same for the woman I am to be
years from now.

To Rise

The first hints of life rise upwards from
frost-bitten dirt,
leaves start to dress once bare branches;
and flowers begin to open to accept the sun.

Oh how long they spent waiting through the icy
darkness of winter,

to rise and bloom again.

www.ingramcontent.com/pod-product-compliance
Lightning Source LLC
LaVergne TN
LVHW010847200726
843508LV00012B/2789